The Bags We Carry

"Harold Recinos testifies to the forgotten, the forsaken, the unseen, and the unrecorded. He is the poet of tamale makers, dish washers, citizens who remember the Mesoamerican sky. His prayers, songs, and tales have an inverse side that can be seen as invectives, demands, and truths. His lyrics are indictments, declarations, and instruments against invisibility. These poems are countermeasures that defy the 'syntax of hate.' They are small sacramental cracks in armor of empire."

—BRUCE SMITH
Author of *Hungry Ghost*

"In *The Bags We Carry*, Recinos offers a collection that is textured, humanizing, and urgent. His poetry makes visible those who are ordinarily invisible in our society, especially those whose dignity is often assaulted by death dealing forces. For Recinos, each poem is an act of prayer, an act of hope, and an act of resistance."

—NICHOLE M. FLORES
Author of *The Aesthetics of Solidarity: Our Lady of Guadalupe and American Democracy*

"With straightforward and compassionate language, these poems rehumanize those who have been repeatedly dehumanized by the rhetoric of those in positions of power and privilege. Recinos bears witness to the systemic injustices of the United States in order to repeatedly and effectively contest what he so rightly calls the 'syntax of hate.' Through surprising juxtapositions and lively line breaks, these pieces invite us to commune with the wino, the Buddha, the *abuela* on her way to church, with Saint Óscar Romero, Billie Holiday, and Maya Angelou, and with the far-flung geographies of El Salvador, Puerto Rico, Florida, and the Bronx all at once, all pulled into the space of the page like a white-hot and urgent prayer."

—JOHN BURNS
Author of *Contemporary Hispanic Poets: Cultural Production in the Global, Digital Age*

"Harold Recinos's poems entwine with a complex but necessary tradition of Spanish Humanism, extending those roots over the structural collapse of national orders and the global consensus that has held those orders, tenuously and often troublingly, in place. In place of that ongoing collapse, Harold Recinos's newest collection of poems, *The Bags We Carry*, abides with the spirit of individual dignity, ethical inquiry, practical faith, and necessary reform. These are poems from a deep philosophical and theological history made for our challenged times."

—EDGAR GARCIA
Author of *Signs of the Americas: A Poetics of Pictography, Hieroglyphs, and Khipu*

"In his newest poetry collection, Harold Recinos's speaker carries with him the literal and symbolic weight of belonging, safety, acceptance, and the search for dignity in the face of fear we live with during these authoritarian times. With Hispanic and minority communities at the forefront of this daring and important book, we—as readers, citizens, activists—are led to question whether it's foolish to 'think God has forgotten the ones who / suffer.' But behind every raid, every corrupt scandal, every morsel of doubt that makes us question our faith, there are *abuelas* armed with an abundance of warmth, strangers extending their callused hands, and music that pours into our souls as though it had come straight from Eden. For every tragedy, *The Bags We Carry* reminds us there is a triumph soon awaiting, and whether we chose to believe in the goodness of humanity or not, under Recinos's lyrical care and narrative arc, we are given a chance to experience 'sweet and gracious love.'"

—ESTEBAN RODRÍGUEZ
Author of *The Lost Nostalgias*

The Bags We Carry

HAROLD J. RECINOS

RESOURCE *Publications* · Eugene, Oregon

THE BAGS WE CARRY

Resource Publications
An Imprint of Wipf and Stock Publishers
199 W. 8th Ave., Suite 3
Eugene, OR 97401

www.wipfandstock.com

PAPERBACK ISBN: 979-8-3852-5271-8
HARDCOVER ISBN: 979-8-3852-5272-5
EBOOK ISBN: 979-8-3852-5273-2

VERSION NUMBER 010526

CONTENTS

SCHOOL DAY

she sat down in the
rocking chair given
to her for Mother's
Day, a favorite song
by Little Anthony on
78 RPM spinning the
harmonies she could
hear every day. then
she rose from the chair
looked at her boy across
the room to say take a
lunch bag to school today
and don't forget to pack
it with dreams.

THE WIND

the birds' songs tremble
this evening pleased with
the cooling air, crickets are
still forming choirs to treat
listeners to their infinite cry
for life and a group of kids
are chasing each other for no
reason. the wind does not have
any color when it reaches the
children at play or brushes the
tiny heads of feathered creatures
witnessing the bubbly hours of
innocent campesino kids. I sit
in a corner wearing the sky like
a big hat and I can almost hear
on this piece of earth heartbeats
waiting for more signs to tumble
into darkened time from God in
heaven.

PANDEMIC

love in the first 21st century
pandemic sees us drift along
each day like patients on the
table waking from an etherized
sleep hoping to hear good news
that the disease introduced to a
new vaccine got lost on its way
to us. I love you in the pandemic,
in days of not knowing when it
will end, in times of quarantine,
and the periods of mystery asking
will the global menace ever end. I
confess nothing can keep me from
noticing the difference you make in
a time of illness.

EXILE

we are the exiles on a
long walk. we are the
tired, the hungry, those
who cannot any longer
weep. we are the people
who sit by the waters of
a river that knows songs
of sadness. we are exiles
with hearts full of village
days far away on the way
to another country pleased
to beat drums of hate. we
hang instruments on weary
Mexican trees rehearsing
lines for those who might
hold us captive in a foreign
land glad to have fled places
that dashed little ones against
the rocks and yearning for a
piece of the world that does
not offer terror and hatred
for strangers.

BROKEN

we are living in a vilifying
country walking backward
and away from widening its
dream. we are living in a land
less free, attracted by religious
intolerance, inspired by hate,
racism, tax breaks for the rich
and no memory for a history of
near Native American genocide,
African enslavement and capital
gain acquired from theft, murder
and rape. we are living in a country
spitting on the huddled masses, the
tired, the poor and dark humanity
yearning to breathe free. we are
living in a country that deceptively
only sees white faces in the American
dream, driven by the foolish idea that
millions of darker newcomers are taking
over things, and where even the most
liberal minded line up to take a turn
dancing around lynching trees. we are
living in a country with churches and
schools not critical about a single damn
thing.

NAME

it is impossible not to smell the damp
Spring morning with the noisy voices
of pigeons gathering on the fire escape,
sunlight coming in the window and the
deep longing in us stirred. mother prays
on her knees in front of a bedroom altar
miles away from where childhood for
her happened, elderly women already
walking the sidewalks yell words into
the ears of children on their way to the
public school with books of Black and
Brown men on the cover and lots of
carefully inked ignorance. it is tiring
telling stories about the invisible people
in the barrio whose cries are unheard,
voices are silenced and chase hope
day after day on the city streets. it is
impossible not to laugh about how we
are now called Latinx in a country that
tells us to go back home though most
of us were born in a city hospital right
here in the USA that still defines us
wetbacks, beaners and spics. someday
the intellectuals employed by colleges
we cannot afford to attend will have
to explain why Tito, Olga and Miguel
are filling up prisons that have never
seen a Latinx person with the wish
to remain silent in a cage.

INVISIBLE

we wake each day to hard
work in harvest fields, meat
packing houses, manufacturing
lines, fast food joints, business
offices, white homes, mowing
grass, cutting trees, repairing cars,
constructing homes, lifting furniture
not owned by us and are daily never
seen. we know ourselves by name,
pray in church, look away from the
news reports that call us dirty things,
experience doors slammed, are scarred
by English slurs tossed about in schools,
courts, the uppity neighborhoods and
even church. we are invisible people
without names, the marginal humanity
unheard, the faceless image in America
of white hate, the Brown men and women
scrubbed from history who live among
those who are citizens who say the words
equality and freedom are not meant for
us.

CIVIL WAR

I think of days sheltered
by the forest, mountain
lanes that called us to the
side of peasants wearing
faces of fright, the bright
language of priests who
were never afraid to talk
about a God of life, and
taking turns declaring the
triumph of love. I think
of staying up to talk until
dawn approached at the
speed of light, dreaming of
a country no longer at war,
loving the moon that threw
kisses our way and the best
of all things was the good
drenching us next to each
other in the dark.

UNWANTED

I am weary of seeing on
the nightly news reports
of ICE masked agents
grabbing immigrants
and nonwhite citizens
profiled by hate. I am
tired of watching images
of officers brutalizing the
innocent while right wing
politicians and Christians
cheer with the president
and his pocket legislators
the trampling of those who
are denied their rights. I
am tired of the felon in
the White House whose
mouth opens and releases
poisonous gas and orders
goose stepping officers that
give dark skinned humanity
reasons to scream. what lesser
memories guide citizens who
do not say no more indigenous
genocide, no more slavery, no
more Auschwitz, Hiroshima,
Wounded Knee, lynching trees
and no more daggers in the
heart of democracy. I am tired
waiting to hear the people say
enough of all this authoritarian
shit.

UNDOCUMENTED

they cut your grass, cook your
food, build your homes, clean
your offices, care for your kids,
rent your apartments, work in
your fields, sleep in crowded
rooms, walk children to school,
pay taxes each day, fear endless
ICE raids and are exceedingly
too weak to weep. they pray in
church, light candles to Saints
and think God will right their
sad days.

EYE OF THE NEEDLE

first, they came for the
undocumented, then the
people with temporary
protected status, then Ukrainian
refugees, then citizens of color,
then political adversaries, then,
women fearlessly speaking, then,
the transgender kids, LGBTQ
humanity, indigenous humanity,
the elderly, teachers, scientists,
doctors, lawyers, clergy, actors,
artists, musicians and people who
are not white national supremacists.
now, they come for you and there
is no one left to protest! now, you
will have a taste of the hate building
walls and the cruelty taking dreams
away in the name of freedom and
white lunacy.

DISGRACE

the barbarism has come with
convenient speeches about the
blood soaked battlefields that
with him will never see living
days of peace. in the decaying
time streaming out of the house
built by slaves, in the city where
half the workforce building the
Capitol building was chained,
a vicious man spends his time
slamming doors, pissing on the
rule of the law and wounding
strangers and fellow citizens by
decree. the perfecting cries of
the discontented never reach him
to move the hatred in his soul
closer to the God some dare to
say choose him. this treacherous
felon sips diet coke in the Oval
Office, while others grieve, his
clothing line is made in Mexico
and ties are manufactured by China
while he screams America first then
strikes a match to cheerfully set her
on fire.

HOUR

I love the quiet night
with lights adorning
trees, clouds floating
past with the silver
moon behind them, a
gentle rain dropping
like tears to rooftops
and the wind sighing
Spanglish words like
they were sent from
heaven. I love when
the dark sky is filled
with stars, naked trees
welcome sparrows, the
scent of Spring flowers
remind me to be with
you in tenderness and
in no other way than
the ways you emerge
in dreams.

FATHER ROGELIO

I knew a priest in the days
of suffering deplored by
the God of the poor who
was always included in the
prayers of campesinos who
saw in him traces of the love
mentioned by the church. he was
raised in Brussels where blood
no longer soaked flowers and
he often held Mass for people
from his parish laid to rest in
silent graves. he walked across
mountains altering prayers with
people in grief, kept up with the
farmers running from soldiers and
denounced the bigoted minds that
ordered helmeted soldiers to leave
villages in mourning. I recall joy
in his voice describing an afternoon
celebrating the Lord's Supper in an
open field surrounded by children,
the elderly and those the news in
America labeled guerrillas. together,
they looked to heaven asking while
breaking tortillas for communion
bread what is precious about life
in places distant from the lights of
the presidential palace and beyond
the reach of militia who make the

innocent bleed and foolishly think
God has forgotten those who
suffer.

NOSTALGIA

I left the year on a hillside
where a shimmering moon
hid the mysteries of life.
with the new year upon us,
I reach for the rosary in my
pocket that belonged to my
mother and nostalgia pushes
me to a tenement passageway
where the Lopez family placed
a neon light on their apartment
door reading, *¡feliz año nuevo!*
I confess it fills me with feelings
of devotion and selfless petitions
for world peace. then, my mind
drifts to the memory of the Jewish
family that lived in apartment 2B
and I could hear the piano in their
living room besting silence with
a song the family played once for
me by the Italian Jewish composer
Salamone Rossi titled "Elohim
Hashiveinu." Lord, may next year,
be extravagantly filled with the will
to find your Holy presence beyond
the places frequented by babbling
idiots.

SPEAK

give voice to the history of
hatred, land theft, violence
and death that began with
the creak of timbers and
Africans enslaved in the
name of white insanity on
land soaked with the blood
of the massacred. give voice
to crimes against humanity,
the cages of the exiled, the
people yelling into the early
dawn, the wounded hardly
mentioned in church, and the
sorrow choked by expensive
bells. give voice to the stories
unrecorded, tales omitted from
founding myths, the language
of the people limping in white
history that still bleeds from sun
up to night. speak of the dark
places unnamed by the strongmen
full of grisly spirits and undreamed
idiocy.

PIETY

I was up early in the morning
in a village scarcely known,
roosters were already singing,
the bread seller was on his bike
making rounds, a few widows
dressed in black with scarves
on graying heads were off to
Mass and a couple of kids were
on the street kicking a soccer
ball between them. last night's
blackness was slowly overcome
with the light of a new day, I leaned
back in a chair to listen to a group
of dogs barking softy and drinking
water from a brook that carved its
way through the valley long before
Spanish was ever spoken on this
piece of the earth. I thought of a
group that visited last night to say
the rosary, sing hymns and gossip
about the long story of God in this
country that still writes love letters
to heaven. I heard a radio played in
the house next door with a woman's
voice giving civil war news interrupted
by station breaks piously saying a day
would come when wolves and lambs
would sit together beneath Ceiba trees.
it occurred to me that the United States

should fly its flag at half-mast for the
poor it spent billions of dollars to crucify
along with their priests.

DETENTION

I visited you after you crossed
the border into a cell, listened
to you weep stories about your
broken family, heard about the
mother and child that drowned
in the river, and wondered out
loud with you about the people
who come from immigrants that
will not let you call this place a
home. you told me that you no
longer believed your slow march
into the shadows was a ticket to
freedom, how speechless stones
remain the only witnesses to the
vigilantes that chased you yelling
"go back to your country" and the
uniformed officials who drove you
to a jail where an ICE officer raped
you. we prayed about exit wounds
and your earth-brown eyes wept of
sadness.

WAITING

I am waiting for the second
coming in a country ignoring
the American dream, listening to
wailing from dark-skinned human
beings crushed by people who think
God is an American. I am waiting
in the shadows with undocumented
women the nationalists call criminal.
I am waiting for a change in people
who just a couple of centuries ago
would have bid for slaves at auction
spots before heading to churches that
make nothing new. I am waiting for a
new day to arrive settled on the corner
with junkies who look for signs of
hope, with Black and Brown children
tired of the sycophantic tales spoken
of them and looking in all directions
for a message of life. I am waiting
for the legislators to stop mopping the
floors of Congress with blood, to stand
up for democracy and demand justice
for the sick, the weak, the poor, the hated
for having dark skin, the Spanish they
speak, the religion they practice and the
dreams they keep.

THE END

keepers of the empire are
boot stomping the ground
in lessening light. they are
near tears since there will
be no brassy military parade
and all the heel clicking they
make will only unsettle the
dusty remains of their piteous
dominion. the words of the
pathological liars are closer
to the time of day when no
one will count their glories.
these people swollen with pride
and spoils acquired from the
slaughtered and chained will
be delivered God says to the
place you cannot take a single
dime with you and they will
for an eternity reap what they
have sowed.

THE NAME

the weary ones who fled
a country no longer theirs,
are those who wash restaurant
dishes, clean offices, harvest
crops, cut meat, mop floors,
care for lawns, construct houses,
press clothing, flip burgers,
take care of sweet kids, fear
ICE raids and question why
in exile they exist speechlessly
with things hidden inside of their
wounds. these people who wear
out God's name with prayers see
fewer signs of the divine around
them and still they believe evil
people with stained hands like
Herod will not see heaven nor ever
understand how hard days unite
the wretched loved by a crucified
God.

TAMALES

wind chimes on the
fifth floor fire escape
were perfectly hung
by the woman who
made tasty tamales
for tenement dwellers
recalling the cornfields
that on windy mornings
leaned in the direction of
a martyred archbishop's
tomb. she could nearly see
the fractured stained glass
windows with damaged
blessed displays that often
made her mother who sat
patiently waiting to taste
the bread of life imagine
liberation is the order of
things to come. she was
known by neighbors on
the block for making the
finest seasonal tamales to
fill tired workers' stomachs
who grind their way with
expectation to murmuring
corners at peace with God
and the storefront church
that caroled, Ave Maria.

HOPE

finding hope away from
home, displaced from the
land of visions, its serene
breezes, cooling ocean and
caring people came down
to this flight to another place
for shelter. the language of
life is inside of us though
in this new world my people
are not free of terror and cruelty
imagined by the loyalists of
bigotry or the politicians who
burn down the sanctuaries
they should cherish. there are
too many jailers here content
to celebrate with their language
of loathing and eager to conceive
ways to pick us apart to make the
work of white nationalist coroners
easy. we have learned after all
these years that in America the
world for many is still quite flat,
truth belongs on the trash heap
and the life of poor dark-skinned
people unwelcome. dear Emily,
you see hope is not a thing with
feathers.

AWAKE

each morning, I play with
birds dancing in an alley,
inhale the smell of freshly
brewed café calling me back
from sleep and the shadows
from last evening's nightmares.
often, I try to remember the
last words spoken by my brother,
mother and prematurely gone
friends that God promised from
the beginning would have no
end. sometimes, glancing at the
branches of a big old tree dark
Angels sitting in them move their
lips. I learned to read them and
they confess to have experienced
more than suggested by Brueghel's
vast snowy expanse and speckled
themes in *The Census at Bethlehem*.
no matter how much time passes, I
never depart the old brick building
in the part of town condemned and
I cannot stop walking with the people
headed to a future not recorded by the
keepers of history.

THE WALK

today, I walked the mile to
public school kicking an ale
can and picking up littered
Lucky Strike cigarette packs
from a cracked sidewalk to
toss in trash cans. it was an
early morning in the Bronx,
young men and women were
up for work and their faces
reflected labor without end.
kids were coming out of the
high-rises that were still the
dwelling places of dreams. I
shouted to Margarita who with
budding brown hair and flash
light eyes was stepping on the
sidewalk. brushing aside her
brown floating hair to disclose
dark eyes she said it would be
fine to make the walk to school
together. only the night before
my eleven-year-old eyes swore
she was surrounded by Angels in
front of the bodega. we walked
that morning past abandoned
buildings, saw junkies on stoops
nodding out, watched two confused
Jehovah witnesses and wondered
what questions the teacher planned
to ask.

HERESY

the people who display
their devotion, prayers
and piety, those who think
their white God makes them
superior on earth should know
this heretically conceived deity
is oblivious to hymns, deaf to
prayers and requires the life of
those dangled like strange fruit
from trees. the people who rip
bread at the altar, who couch the
world in the darkness of lunatics
are plagued by delusions that say
a dark-skinned savior lynched to
a tree ignores the pleas of those
crushed on earth. the people who
believe God only has white sons
and daughters need a little more
wisdom to know in heaven there is
no favorite whitish nation tradition
to endorse.

SANTERA

on hot sunny days she
never bothered to listen
to the screaming on the
streets favoring to walk
with an umbrella over her
head. on Home Street no
one doubted she was light
for darkness and even the
winos on the block sipping
Midnight Express were told
by her that inside their cheap
drink there was a sacrament
waiting to rise like a genie
from a bottle. she spent nights
in the botanica presenting souls
to the African God Chango who
everyone knew never set foot in
the Presbyterian church on Tiffany
Street. Chango knew all the young
mothers that cut off the heads of
Saints kept in their bedrooms for
not granting prayers in this harsh
country.

DRUNKARD

I have seen more untruthful
things in the past eight years
than abuelas dreamed on fire
escapes on windy Autumn
nights. I have listened to
tales from men and women
who walked across the desert
to a block called home. I have
sat on stoops with kids admitting
people who carried wounds for
centuries, bleed. I have come to
understand the country that wants
to break my bones, remove my
eyes and dangle me from a tree
cannot silence my people with
hate, keep them quiet in graves,
nor stop the approaching hope,
justice and peace. I have sat in
morning hours with a retreating
moon casting light on Hank the
wino sleeping it off leaving me
wondering about the pearly gates
opening for people on forsaken
streets.

THE FIRE ESCAPE

I overheard them on the
fire escape that afternoon
talking about living long
like trees, laughing when
squirrels ran the sidewalks,
and smiling at pigeons tending
their young. I concluded these
Spanglish children are the angels
talked so much about in churches
that gossip about God. I heard
them laughing at little Willy who
was crossing the street wearing
a pair of trousers nearly sagging
by his knees and it was clear to
me they knew happiness right
near.

OUR LADY OF SORROWS

every Sunday we dressed to
head to the basement of the
Catholic church that spoke
only Spanish. the abuelas
attended wearing black lace
scarfs over their heads to tell
God who never posed for the
lovely stained glass window
they cared. we loved sitting
in the pews with fine threads
that would even have made
Jesus look unfashionable on
a bench. I could not keep
from staring at the morning
light making its way into the
church basement that looked
something like the sanctuary
upstairs where shadows were
chased away by hundreds of
candles burning for Saints on
watch. I always thought the
church was misnamed Saint
John Chrysostom believing
with the old women in the
basement that we preferred
Our Lady of Sorrows just
because she walked with us
and could always be found
in lowly places comforting
the poor.

THE WITNESSES

the Jehovah witnesses
are knocking on the door
eager to call us out to hear
their subsidized message.
we open the door to tell a few
stories of our own about God
unfamiliar in their watchtower
and straight from hungry stomachs
in the apartment. they knocked on
the door with the Sacred Mother
decal wanting to share words and
not offering any bread. we listened
carefully to them share the belief
that Jesus did not die on the cross
but on a single wood stake. we told
them instead Jesus dies every day
on the block and saves us around
the corner in a storefront church led
by an ex-junkie whose words rise
from the demolished buildings on
Mapes Avenue.

DAWN

it was dawn on the street
and an old woman walked
with ease on the way to Mass
at a church that listened to
her confession for over twenty
five years. I could see on her
wrinkled face the lonely street
held memories for her of walking
in her lovers arms, skipping with
her children, and recollections of
dreams shared with a partner who
departed to a place of unending
silence. sometimes in Mass, I
would see her with closed eyes
withdrawing into her sadness
fondling white rosary beads. I
thought, surely after the service
God delivered her to the ground
where her beloved lay.

EL BALCON

I am going to the Balcony
club tonight to lean back
in a chair to pay attention
to songs that were lifetime
achievement awards once
for singers unforgotten in
note floating spaces. I may
even imagine musicians in
the room joined by the ghost
of Charlie Parker breathing
melodies from his alto sax
turning the tavern into a jazz
haven. I will open my eyes wide
to the sound of blues that leave
feelings dangling from rafters
in the room and traveling down
wet cheeks to strangely offering
comfort. I will sit with sparkling
water absorbing the incantation
from the drums, guitar, bass and
human voice and feel the walls
shaking in ways the Holy Ghost
could not this night match.

STROLL

I will go for a walk down
the block counting lamp

posts to find sleep, with
time racing helplessly

ahead of itself, putting
aside the avalanche of

lies that overflow from
the mouth of a truculent

toddler nearer 80 than
three. on this evening

walk just a few blocks
will suffice to think deeply

about the people who believe
after a long journey from south

of the border the earth has
common cause with them,

rather than the rich fat man
full of hate, the lost cause

and swastikas in his bedside
table. I will walk until my eyes

are heavy and find a time to
laugh at the loser who offers

fans improvised bullshit, while
I gossip with others that he can't

stop the expected future.

THE STEPS

I sit on the building steps
watching the kids play
mythical games given
to them by elders from
El Salvador and Guatemala.
they charge down the sidewalk
avoiding cracks, now and
again, pausing to stare into
an alley where Eddy spaghetti
like Narcissus stares into a
window admiring his good
looks. pigeons are flying
above their heads like the
unfettered Torogoz called
by the guides at the Bronx
Zoo the Turquoise-browed
motmot. unexpectedly, an
old woman leans out of the
second floor window yelling
Willie do not forget to bring
home pan francés from la
bodega.

GUEST

the god who helped us
cross rivers is leaning
against the building wall
tonight, encouraging us
to pray for rain to water
dry mouths with lips still
trembling with memories
of the desert. the god who
walked with us did not expect
to hear us chant songs carried
for hundreds of miles with dreams
swelling in this new country that
despises us.

WHITE FLIGHT

the Fuller Brush salesman was
knocking on doors in the building
dressed with white side of town
gray suit. he was carrying a large
bag full of products. my mother
got a look at him through a door
peephole and mumbled surprise
seeing a pale faced man showing
up on a quiet afternoon to pitch a
sale of cleaning brushes and twisty
things with a big English speaking
smile. I could see she was unsure
about opening the door though after
a long minute she slid the police
lock, turned the handle on the bolt
latch, opened the door saying ¿si?
I tried to understand the look on
the man's face when Spanish reached
his pink ears, then I concluded after
a deal shattered into tiny pieces, he
he will wonder for days where the
white folks who lived in the building
went.

THE BLUES

the music poured into the
room with more than a few
regulars swaying to sounds
rising in them with memories
made of dreams. the dim lights
trembled slightly above a stage
drumming joyful beats for the
weary sliding into an evening in
Eden!

THE MIRACLE

you were born in the days
of early Spring with your
mother chanting the ways
she loves you. nurses heard
her say she intended giving
you an English name, rather
than one from the list of names
that came from her dismantled
Spanish colonial empire. you
experienced a first breath at the
margins of this metropolis, in
the belly of a rich city working
the poor into premature graves,
in that part of the world believed
to have offensive dark-skin, a
filthy non-English language and
nothing but hundreds of Latinx
poor. in the misty apartment you
went to live, the little kids on the
second floor came to see you in
a crib and they smiled.

LIES

it was a hot night
in the late Fall when
news reached me like
a silvery moon making
its way with dim light
into the wettest places
inside my heart. I heard
another twist of lies saying
ugly things of migrants
for the benefit of all the
people for whom truth
does not matter. I wanted
to ring the news shows to
tell them about the good
prayers of uprooted human
beings, the ones who never
see borders on maps. I wanted
to talk of the villagers who fled
homes, their evenings of whispered
talk and sad eyes playing their part
conjuring memories of a world
of violence, murder and rape. I
wanted to shout these are God's
children no matter what politicians
pitching white lies say.

REMEMBER

do you remember the
unnamed dogs roaming
the alley where the old
Jewish violinist played
and money rained down
from windows. let me
remind you of the times
you promised kneeling
at an altar rail to be good,
how you swore to Fr. Rossi
you would not throw rocks
at squirrels that lived down
by the creek and you would
talk to your brother about the
needle stuck in his veins. I bet
you often think of the hooky
parties held in the basement
listening to Motown hits and
slow dancing with girls you
got around the city with on
foot. I know the memories
are heavy to carry but your
Brown face lights up when
you tell stories worthy of being
turned into carols for American
radios to play.

OVERDOSE

we are made from the
clay of the earth not
for walking in counsel
with the wicked, to find
streams flowing in the
desert, to weep for those
chasing vain things and
to pray to heaven about
fears. from Holy rooftops
where the city's sins appear,
we are called to pray until
your thorned head nods, yes.
we wept when Joey overdosed
in the arms of another junkie,
thanked You for chasing terror
from our souls and welcomed
your promise that death has no
sting in the context of your sweet
and gracious love.

THE MASS

on winter Sundays,
my mother was up
preparing café with
her tired cracked
hands in the kitchen
listening to her favorite
Spanish radio station. I
would slowly wake from
a night thick with dreams
to hear her moving dishes
and singing along with Celia
Cruz tunes pushing their way
out of a tiny radio above the
stove. I would get out my
best clothes and hardly worn
Sunday shoes to accompany
this hardworking woman to
worship. she was in the habit
of praying with grand devotion
though I was inclined to think
God in heaven not answering
prayers didn't understand a word
of Spanish.

GAMES

we ran streets with the
locura expected from
Pentecostals worked
into frenzy and dancing
the aisles of a storefront
church. the dreams we
carried made the rounds
with us, keeping step with
screams and beyond reach
for the cops showing up to
turn off unauthorized living
in us. we played in fire hydrant
water refreshing weary bodies
with more than a few of the
kids who emerged from the
alley to join the games after
sniffing glue in Perez bodega
number two brown bags. we
eagerly chased each other up
and down the street, yelling
and cursing and not a single
cop from the 41st Precinct could
prevent the bliss.

BORDERLANDS

history older than a guarded
border allows us to recall
El Valle, barefoot children,
bridges on Latinx backs,
colonias despised and the
cost of Brown dreams. we
know the borderlands ignored
by churches, defined by a white
world contemptuous of truth,
death in deserts, on ranchos and
cliffs. we see the shooters who
lurk on the north side of the
artificial line who carry white
supremacist beliefs in little
hearts and imagine lynching
Brown human beings made in
the image of God. we crossed
the border and stopped at a
chapel for those who suffer
and people lighting candles in
it whispered Texas leads in
mass shootings and that does
not account for the undocumented
lives disappeared on the land of
purple mountain majesty.

HUMAN BEINGS

Ana wants you to know
we are human beings with
beautiful Brown skin, eyes
that tear, hands that callous,
hearts that entreat, not white,
not rich, only human from first
to last. we escaped the world
that once enslaved us, a place of
violence, poverty, death, greed
and terror. we have come to the
cradle of shattered bodies, a place
races are pitted against each other,
the star-spangled home of lynch mobs
and killer cops who love nothing more
than seizing us. Ana wants you to
know we are human beings baptized
in the name of Christ, singing your
damn translated hymns, presenting
exaggerated looks of captivity and
screaming for acts of kindness from
you.

RESTAURANT

we struggled to walk with
lighted candles on a path in
the park. beneath the stars,
we replayed the night Julia
was found in the bathroom
of a Chinese Restaurant in
which she shot dope into
a vein for the last time. the
weight of her departure was
like a boulder coming down
on our heads. the candles
burning were not meant to
magnify God but to help us
find a way out of the darkness
into bearable Eden. we walked
the footpaths in the little park,
we confessed to the sacred Lady
of Sorrows and prayed for Julia
to be finally embraced in a place
she can do no wrong.

THE WILL

last night, in a dream
I wrote a last testament
requesting to have my
ashes scattered from a
mountain top into the
air that knows nothing
of doors, walls, money
and divisions. I wanted
to find rest sprinkled in
that sweet space holding
the poor who never shake
in chains, where departed
friends float among the
clouds and find thousands
of ways to still play and
yell about what is beautiful.
I wanted my ashes spread
where God picks flowers,
makes water run in deserts
and has a piece of freedom
waiting for me.

VOTE

we have seen elections come
and go, inauguration days with
leaders declaring to defend the
common good, and others who
stroll home after expressing
lies, glad to serve the interests
of agents from other countries
who have the goods on them. we
have lived for democracy from
the beginning, seen the canyons,
walked the forests, mountains,
vast prairies, cities, suburbs,
and villages. we have seen
the waves from sea to shining
sea appear and still the small
voice asks will the ballot box
deliver us from the dark days
that give us too many reasons
to worry. in any voting season,
we are the ones that count so
why not break down the door
for equality, truth and freedom?
why not disrupt the silence and
drape a divided America with a
new canopy of dreams?

THE SCHOOL

you thought it easy to
ask questions of the sixth
grade teacher after leaving
the assembly hall where the
Black and Brown kids from
the block pledged allegiance
to the flag. when we walked
the ten blocks to school the
teachers eagerly received us
with school lessons they carried
like stacked books kept in
another world held together
by white glue. one afternoon
I had the nerve to say people
who live on my block never
came by way of Ellis Island
and not one of them arrived
to steal work. I said many
have experienced miserable
days working on farms harvesting
lettuce used in the Caesar's salads
dished up in the restaurant in the
park called the Tavern on the
Green. my sixth-grade teacher
allowed me to speak, then I asked
her to explain the meaning of purple
mountain majesty without ignoring
she had a full classroom of bruised
Spanglish kids yearning to breathe
free.

THE KITE

dreams on the rooftop were
like the cheap kites made of
paper with raggedy tails and
flown on fishing line. they fly
above the city streets and are
made by little kids who scream
on rooftops with unrestricted delight.
On kite days there comes a time
to finally demand the floats with
tails made from old tee shirts
and bed sheets be cut free and
the kids watch them glide away
freely to a different world.

ISLA DEL ENCANTO

Puerto Ricans have fought in
your wars for what? we have
wasted tyrants for whom? we
have been fatally overworked
until blood oozed from every
colonized pore? why the suffering
in chains for your white God?
with tears rolling down our
cheeks we see the faces of Saints,
the cruelty of crushed dreams
and slumped flags on soldiers'
coffins, public schools, courtrooms
and Black and Brown souls with
stars and stripes with holes. my
people have learned to carry their
own light down the road and away
from the piety of hate, the suffocating
colonialism and the ugliness of
a world promising enlightenment
and reformed Christian hymnals
saturated with the experiences
of a white Protestant male worldview
that has tried for more than a century
to turn us into modern day slaves.

WINTER

on the street in the early
winter morning, the old
lampposts slowly turning
off, the front page of a day
old newspaper blown like
ash down the block, I came
out of the alley where I
slept in darkness and was
alone on the sidewalk. I
counted it a blessing not
having to rise to dress like
others living in apartments,
I only had one set of clothes
with me for sleep in the alleys,
the abandoned buildings, down
by the creek or a trailway bus
parked on the whiter side of the
city. sometimes, I roamed the lower
east side with other unwelcome Puerto
Rican kids themselves as American
as the Great Migration from the South,
mom's apple pie and the café con leche
never enough to drink.

THE RUNNERS

on the rolling hills and flat
stretches of road they swing
their arms with slightly closed
fists and feet moving quickly
to catch them before they fall.
these runners carry thoughts
concealed within each step
swiftly taken for the sake of
joy instead of fame. they fly
by roaring crowds, laughing
children, ripening flowers
and cops directing traffic
without frowns. their steady
feet return the onlookers to
mysteries hinted in moving
things and they manage to
take us to a whole new world
of freedom.

YEAR OF THE DRAGON

in this year of the Dragon
the nature deity that soars
earth and skies, roaming in
the fog and rising from the
deep waters with the sun, we
sat around the table in China
town imagining the auspicious
arrival of this creature that was
towed across seas by Chinese
hearts longing to melt away the
walls blocking different times
for basking in dreams making
better sense of the world. the
long tail on this creature is like a
bench for ancestors, immigrants
from elsewhere, people beyond
the memory of these shores with
lives that matter. it is impossible
to forget this Autumn evening, the
moon casting light on this piece of
the rolling earth and the many ways
the mythic creature from a distant
world makes a home within us to
bewitch the moment enough to
open hearts widely around the
dinner table.

ELECTION

learning to hold on to hope
in a wide-open world is more
than a thing with feathers. it
may be the brightness leaning
into a fresh day, sobbing that
interrupts silence, the nearness
of a suffering God and imagined
winged things. it may simply be
the day memorized in America
with freedom, the long walk to
the promised land, spitting on
the twisted Bibles thrown by
white hands at the weary and
a White House that will not
listen. when the shade is thin,
the light stands up to darkness
and nights are colder after the
election day. hope you see is
not believing the old man afraid
of democracy who hoards loaves
and fishes for himself.

ALONE

I have been sitting with a dim
light alone thinking about the
homeless days that left my soul
blemished, yearning for bread,
thirsty for water to soothe the
dry knots in my throat, unable
to stop the weeping provided
to me by hearts of stone that
called me worthless spic. you
see, from childhood hours in
the slums I knew alone, in the
knee-deep exile from Nuyorican
corners, the lashes taken when
roaming a white world, in my
visits to counterfeit churches
with outstretched hands left
empty, I have known what it
means to be alone. tonight, on
God's earth I will sit in the dark
thinking of following a turning
river with signs on its shores
reading beloved you made it
to mysterious Eden.

THE DAY AFTER

the darkness will not sleep
quietly with glittering stars
shining brightly for us after
election day. the scratched
veins of democracy bleed
and many citizens weep and
and gossip about the apathy
for human decency and the
perfectly planned funeral for
democracy's end. we have
seen this day coming for many
months, heard the chanting on
the streets, witnessed inhumanity
for dark-skinned border crossers,
perceived the inequality of women,
violence for gay humanity and
the nation trying shamelessly to
cover the sun. tonight, rejoice in
the darkness and feel no despair
for the lunacy of the psychopathic
goose-steppers mesmerized by
bullshit who will know soon enough
to choose a better future or march
into a grave.

THE TOURNAMENT

they leaped, twisted, turned
and landed routines uttering
no more than a few sentences
that wished each day could be
made so beautifully by artful
play. I heard elderly spectators
cheering kids say the world
is too perfect and no one would
dare finish it. the players spent
weeks preparing in front of mirrors,
learning patterns to make their
own. the audience clapped for them
performing various sequences to
to set the spirit free, and the crowd
was carried to some kind of heaven
by the beauty of bodies floating over
old wood floors demonstrating the
movements that originated in the
complex messages birthed by the
mysteries of ancient souls.

BLESSING

darkness pushes away
light but cannot keep
the eye from beginning
to see down the length
of the winding path to
the places where birds
are already bunched to
sing. I heard abuelas
sitting on the stoop say
God enters the darkness,
glides with fierce wind
and reminds us not to allow
unheavenly things to sway
us to lend deaf ears to the
phrase, "do not be afraid."
let us hurry in the days
ahead to find kindness in
the shadows, love taking
us by the hand, divinity in
the saddest times and places.
today, let us remember hope
waits tirelessly for us.

PRAISE

when I am walking on Avenue D
on the Lower East Side reading the
graffiti tagging the project walls like
masterpiece paintings, I feel wind
blowing through the spaces between
buildings from the East River, catch
the scent of food carried from open
windows into the streets like bread
offered by Christ at the welcoming
table and I think in the darkest of
times preferred by hurt human beings
who breathe stale barrio air on the
truth will go on. I sometimes lose
my bearings on these walks, find
street musicians on corners singing
to remind me the future being snap
shut in the name of hate is not mine,
the heavy load of life outside of God's
moral universe cannot keep anyone
down for long nor will times of cruelty
and violence prevent facts from finding
new ways to bind us with love.

WORD

freedom will never trip
in darkness, stay quiet
while lunacy runs its
course nor accept one
day with fear. it will have
us stand on two feet like
the proud builders of life
in sumptuous diversity
and with amplest care. we
have the truth and all the
troubled people on our
side. remember on the
next uneasy night to resist
the gloom, the dreadful
feeling the practices of
love are dead. find God
with that aching heart deep
within you punching holes
in blackness shouting see
there is light.

NIGHT

in the night, we think
about how we live, the
periods of happiness are
recalled more than once,
questions raised remain
unsolved, the hypocrites
pushed out of mind, relentless
news cast aside and peace
with the mysterious grace
that roams the earth rushes
in to set us free.

BOOK FAIR

the book fair that rolled
into town stretched for
several blocks, volumes
adorned tables trusted
with stories beloved by
children and the literary
tourists that came to visit.
the tents shielded the dreams
we carry to places familiar
and unknown. crowds filled
the tents, people mingled
with each other, they shared
smiles, passing exchanges
and the fair showed itself a living
thing with a universal language
God would find pleasing. I did
not see the two-headed calf, the
six-legged goat or a scary haunted
house on a back street, instead
they lingered around the whole
day in the books delighting the
imagination of strollers.

FINE

the act of kindness from
a recovered alcoholic in
a Florida town is largely
unremembered by friends,
the people who attended
can't-help-you churches or
by the light that a silvery
moon managed time and
again to share. I recall
the AA man in dreams, still
hear him speaking softly to
a room full of recovering
alcoholics and drug abusers
like a mother singing sweet
lullabies to a troubled kid.
the promises of God were
somehow planted inside of
this man who felt the world
was offered once again to
his tearful imagination in
a recovery meeting that was
a space to read sweet psalms.
I will never forget his simple
act of kindness in a room with
reformed drunks who pooled a
few cents for the man to buy a
bus ticket for a homeless kid
from Jacksonville to New York
City.

AGING

each year delivers another
wrinkle that drops in without
broadcasts from unfolding
time. different truths begin
to occupy us, the memory
weakens and our hearts are
splendidly delighted to feel
the passing seasons. we spend
time like keeping score of how
many passengers climb aboard
to be carried by aging bodies
hiding innocent children within.
we have been given years to
dream in worlds that contain
too little love and in places
where not a single wrinkle can
remove the optimism rolling
like pebbles in the soul.

CRY ALOUD

the wind weeps in the country
I love and lunatic explanations
are offered for the blood soon
to spill on holy ground. there
is weeping on corners tonight
for the promised futures about
to be destroyed by government
laughing you plainly see at those
who cry aloud. what comes is
not the doing of those who feel
white supremacy lashing the
country forgetting its democracy,
decency, equality and freedom.
the wind howls summoning the
trampled to sing hymns with the
undocumented masses who have
exquisite dreams for a torn nation
nearer to vanishing from sea to
sea.

THANKSGIVING

we give thanks for gathering
to share bread, for blessings
in unfair time, the fragrance
of Autumn in shady days, the
love of family and friends to
make a feast. we give thanks
for grace that hears the need
in prayer, for the church bells
that ring near and in the season
delivering the sweet blessings
of things. we give thanks for
the houses full of light, for the
good places calling us to them,
the Holy eyes looking down on
us and for all the days to come
grateful for joys and tears. we
give thanks for not believing
the lies narrated about the
United States and for recalling
thanksgiving as a day of cheer
and indigenous sorrow. we give
thanks for the moon rising over
the earth, for not losing kindness
and beauty born from everything
unseen.

DRUMMER

shorty walked around most
days with drumsticks used
to play on garbage can tops,
milk crates, cracked steps
and greasy art deco chairs
in the restaurant owned by
Gilberto's father. one night
siting on the building steps
listening to the salsa radio
show called symphony Sid,
shorty said he was inspired
by the drummer for a group
no Puerto Rican on the block
knew that went by the name
The Monkees. it was the first
time the kids paused to hear
about white music shorty said
was sweet with mystery. this
pinch me kid thickened the story
about The Monkees with his
voice rising balloon-like when
he talked about the white band
like they just dropped in on the
block from heaven.

GRIEF

after the launch of
childhood in a part
of the city burning, near
the Hoe Avenue Peace
meetings calling for an
inter-gang alliance and
truce, beyond the spot
where the viejos played
congas, where diseased
trees had branches over
the avenue, the street
stretched passed the white
part of town, and the block
kids leapt over cracks on
the sidewalk, we watched
distant stars until your
days came to an end not
long after celebrating your
31st year. I have discharged
the grief that trotted into me
like horses and blamed God
in distant heaven. after decades,
I confess the divine mute has
occasionally touched me with
a gentle hand allowing grief
to fall from my eyes like rain.
mourning betrays me often in
church when I sit with Our Lady
of Guadalupe asking the Sacred
Mother to care for you.

THE SEASON

the morning is full of
sounds in the late Fall,
Christmas lights begin
to appear on lampposts,
a cross-town wind passes
waving to kids playing on
the sidewalk, words from
many languages are thrown
to the fifth floor and a girl
with oceanic eyes looks out
of a window. in this barrio,
the unfolding season gathers
love like things in an aging
tenement, sadness becomes
like water poured on nets
that cannot hold it, stories
are shared into the evening
on stoops, in bodegas, seated
on church pews, in kitchens
and places where the light is
bright. perhaps, God is not so
far, the moon sings and hearts
imagine peace far beyond any
experience.

IN THESE TIMES

darkness cannot stand
light shining on it, the
hollow ethic of all the
sycophants, the palaces
of kings that are painted
with blood, the rich gorging
on misery and greed sinking
a nation into the depths of
hell. let us pray for darkness
to turn the corner sharply in
the years to come, to disappear
like other empires and brand the
the brows of those who will never
cross the Jordan into the promised
land of former slaves. light will
make the culture of cruelty a stale
stench of waste to be written in
books, presented on news shows
and confessed on the social media
platforms like sin.

THE PLUNGE

we drove down the mountain
heading back to the house in
the village, shots were not
fired, helicopters did not fly
over the road dropping bombs
and it was clear that in civil war
love is not bankrupt. it is a thing
that endures divisions and in
seasons of war still sings. I recall
the ride to the valley was quick,
sweet words passed between us,
friends lost on the front were in
us and we prayed in the old car
with faulty breaks to God who
was yet trying to make us Holy
with words. love, it occurred
to me listening to a cumbia on the
car's radio, should not end like the
flames dancing on church candles
in Romero's Cathedral.

THE PICTURE

when I was seven my mother
hired a photographer to take
pictures of her two sons in new
outfits like they were about to
appear on a white television show.
she offered prayers the night before
to Saints on a bedroom altar that
were adorned with flowers and a
few rosaries blessed in the local
church by the same priest who
baptized her boys whom she gave
American names. all that time
between picture day and today,
I have missed laughing with my
brother, diving into the familiar
pattern of my mother's dreams
and spending each day rearranging
the world to fit the Puerto Rican
imagination I learned in a single
room apartment. I was taught to
recite the names of Saints made
from clay and I still carry a copy
of an original picture of the suspender
boys. I have carried the photo since
the days of sleeping on cardboard on
the rooftops of abandoned tenements
and today it rests in a university desk
drawer.

THE SANDBOX

he reached the yard, dumped
the plastic bucket filled with
toy trucks in his hand and ran
over the side of a big sandbox
dashing around in it from corner
to corner like it was the desert
only this time a playground for
kids. the look in his glad eyes
made teachers on the playground
smile and gossip about his mother
who walked with him for weeks
trembling in flight and over the
unknown life in the Bronx. the
boy was content to play bare
footed laughing in the sandbox
with the kid who was missing
a hand taken by a gang in El
Salvador. they were children
with Spanish names, dark like
the earth with kind faces who
reminded the rest of the world
to pay attention to the innocent
lives offering more hints about
kindness and God than a Sunday
Bible study.

SWIMMING HOLE

beneath the train bridge
stretching into midtown
Manhattan with suburban
passengers headed to work,
a part of the sea has fled to
form a bit of the East River,
it listens to the confessions
of kids who plunge into its
depths, guards floating logs
used to drift by the boys who
read Tom Sawyer and is a haven
far from the shrieking sirens of
the 41st Precinct police. the block
gang could always be found by the
river enjoying what they oddly called
the quiet life, whispering about Lelo's
father who was a municipal garbage
man who marched each year in the
Puerto Rican Day parade and imagining
the Manger displayed for Advent at the
Catholic church on Hoe Avenue with a
Holy Family harmless like their own in
the apartments with dark skin. these kids
playing in the currents were familiar with
Our Lady of the Bronx River to whom they
sang bent notes made from the riotous games
forbidden in churches that had forgotten the
gospel.

CONFESSION

the priest
in the
confessional
was never
indifferent
to
words
shared with
him
in a dark
time
by people
who spoke
in a low
voice
in the
basement
of the
church.
sometimes,
a bitter voice
spread
like
leaves
on
grass
in Crotona Park
to
lighten
the load

of tearful
old
men and
women
who knew
the
names
of
Saints.

TREE LIGHTING

I saw pale children wearing shoes
from a bin at Catholic charities in
the park for the lighting of the big
Christmas tree. they smiled at each
other grateful in advance that a few
presents may reach them before the
new year. I saw mothers speaking to
each other in Spanish about getting
together to make pupusas to feed
skinny kids and saying out loud
darkness comes fast at this time of
the year. I saw grandmothers on a
bench whispering to each other how
the tree reminds us to pray each day
for light, expressing their anxiousness
for peace and wondering whether they
would laugh next year. I saw crowds
admiring the Christmas tree wondering
how many have related cruel times to
history, faces in the nation dimmed by
hate and the happiness that the White
House will never flower.

CROWDED ROOM

in the beginning there
was light in the single
room apartment with a
Puerto Rican flag nailed
to a bedroom wall. the
lightbulb dangling from
a beige ceiling enveloped
the three kids who slept in
the room with cheerfulness and
often revealed particles of dust
floating around. the bedroom
lacked furniture other than three
beds placed beside each other
in a perfect row, a chair used
by a mother who occasionally
entered the room at night to tell
stories of growing up on the island
of enchantment, tales colored by
love and innocence, narratives that
shined their way into innocence. it
is impossible to forget the memories
of first light that overcame darkness
in that space, how the poor woman
knew how to love and the way they
see her now in the wind, the leaves
blown by the park wind, on the faces
strolling sidewalks and in every little
bit of light untouched by contempt.

SPANGLISH

pues, I will spend a
little tiempo creando
Spanglish that reflects
the culture contacto de
mundos muy different
abrazando in the barrio
in the name of migrants,
salsa, bachata, mambo,
hip hop, abuelitas, and
todo el slang que esta
on the corner. tal vez,
you know algo of this
inter-textual lengua de
the young born pledging
allegiance to Tio Sam
and existentially wired
like the Nuyorican kids
que pasan la noche in the
poets café. coño, there are
no mango trees on the old
bloque, Papo has not seen
a ceiba since he visited his
mother in El Salvador and
yo ando buscando quien
vive debajo the floor boards
in building 1203.

TROUBLE

we have trouble with
us longer than God has
been around, making
us brace whenever
somebody in church
shouts out lies. we
can't bury them deep,
send them up the street,
see them off to school
like kids. before running
out of time, we hope for
a day trouble just can't
find.

THE WHINER

will the truth leak out
with remarkable content
into newspapers, podcasts,
television and photos taped
to lampposts? will story ink
stain the fingers turning the
pages of magazines idolizing
the crooked, the reckless, the
perjurers, the grifters and the
people full of shit? what are the
pious men and women saying
about the wrangling tongue of
the declining sexual predator
who sold his mug shot to cash
strapped idiots and became a
face on a magazine preposterously
alleging a bigoted, misogynist, sex
offending, xenophobic, supremacist,
philanderer and serial liar should
be called person of the year. perhaps,
it should be made clear that we do
not believe in bullshit tossed about by
the propaganda machine defending
an unaccomplished buffoon, his bully
pulpit and malevolent vision of God.

THE RIDE

I saw a field of flowers
in her hair driving down
the mountain, the whirling
earth circling her head like
rabbits, her slender dark hand
moving between rosary beads
and night laying back for a tiny
while more to allow her radiant
face a place in the world to sink
shadows. perhaps, time will halt
its forward march once we reach
the laughing valley and we will be
carried backward to a mysterious
paradise where aches are shed.

HOMELAND

my homeland is a despised
piece of a northern country
where a part of me remains
alive. it was not invaded by
soldiers paid by a foreign land
to kill, it was occupied instead
by dope coming from overseas
to settle on the street corners and
lives turned into nightmares. I
often think about my country,
the rooftop where Joseph died,
the corner where the Bosco kids
were stabbed, the cops that beat
Tito for no reason with knife sticks
making him bleed, the men running
for political office standing in front
of abandoned buildings and lots of
politicians making promises they knew
were impossible to keep and churches
on every other block spitting out lots
of indecipherable prayers that offer
the poor nothing to eat. days for me
often include walking around these
memories like a sunny morning stroll
hearing the wild laughter of little kids.
in my homeland, we bitterly stand to
sing the national anthem wearing a
crown of thorns.

ODIUM

I pity those who walk around
full of hate. they keep in shape
detesting those they will not allow
into the future and only imagine
others white like them. I pity the
people who craft sentences about
making America white again and
remain unaware their spiraling
planet was created with luxurious
diversity. I pity the men in power
in dark rooms fighting the battles
of the lost cause, the moral emptiness
of bootlickers who rape the truth
and stomp on people they believe
inferior to them. I pity citizens
who wear white hoods after church
and reek of obscenity. I pity people
with barren thoughts in their stoned
hearts that keep them from praying
on their knees to God who will slap
them with a Black hand and ask them
in Spanish to repent.

SPIRITS

I have called upon the old
spirits that roam cobblestone
streets making appearances
late at night. theologies have
not made any sense of them
though I never become tired
of their dazzling radiance on
138th street by Cypress Avenue
where kids still gather for a little
mischief. they are the ones who
have carried the words of the
barrio to a non–English speaking
God who offers a manifesto on
injustice that rests on a podium in
the Catholic church going by the
name, Bible. they answer slowly
when they arrive with gentle breezes
that tell the stories stirring in them,
timelessly. it has taken me all these
years to understand whispering to
is like prayer that catches tears, so
I ask the spirits to come around the
tenements full of weeping.

THE SEASON

it is a week before Christmas,
the poor are shipping north
to cities soon to be engulfed
with snow they have never
experienced. they will settle
in urban barrios to find God
could not be detained in the
villages they fled and they
will kneel before the One
who lets justice fall from
heaven to remove the thorns
plunged into Brown flesh by
misguided clowns. the carolers
are in the tenement standing
in front of open doors singing
O Come All Ye Faithful to the
Newcomers who cannot speak
English though are not hesitant
to smile.

CREATION

I am the wooden bridge over
the dead river rushing by the
cardboard houses resting on
its banks. I know the poor who
survive time reciting prayers
empowering them to resist one
more day. I know from the kids
playing soccer that love is laughter
on the streets not distracted by wounds.
I know people who have never walked
on water, spend years swimming on
land and marching in protests to unveil
the thick secrets of an unjust world. I
know like Maya why caged birds must
sing loud enough to be heard in distant
hills. I know the sound of footsteps in
the village at dawn, the church bells that
ring each morning, my ears hearing voices
from the Shanty town where Maria lives
reciting new petitions for God in heaven
who listens. I know the woodpecker that
lives in the neighborhood tree, the spider
that with a filament of silk sails to safer
ground. I know how to be still enough to
keep my soul in a world with a language
that touches me.

NATIVITY

I gathered gifts in my
arms from the tired in
the tenement, junkies,
old men with little faith,
and abuelas who dust
Saints. I carried them to
the nativity scene in front
of the church looking up
at the bell tower begging
the infant for love to come
from above for the unseen
who think of paradise like a
peaceful night in the weary
city.

REDEMPTION

nothing was ever certain
when the birds stopped
singing and daylight was
wrestled away earlier than
expected. the little village
turned its back on us and
the walk in the wilderness
no matter the libations tipped
for the dead delivered us to
a neighborhood with drunks
who never mattered for the
rich. we came with many
stories to tell, memories of
hiding in secret spaces and
talk about what bullets can
do to women and children
who never mattered in accounts
of the civil war. things have
changed a little though tenement
life at the edges of the city reminds
us of days hiding from soldiers.
the world of white lies manages
to disappoint the hope carried
by us from thousands of miles
but we never stop praying for
God to redeem us.

THE BELLS

the bells of Christmas ring
familiar carols, gifts beneath
the tree, the pews singing glory
everywhere and on this glad
day on earth God's peace
seen on an infant's face. on
Christmas day, the poor, the
hungry, the ill, the imprisoned,
and all who need the Word made
flesh confess evidence plainly
reveals the dislocated Mary
and Joseph with a newborn
babe sent from heaven to an
occupied land is here to take the
world by love. now, we strike up
music the swapping gifts and
church bells declare an odd beauty
arrived on earth saying the prince
of peace comes to break chains,
scatter the mighty from their thrones
and send wrong empty away. Amen!

THE JUNGIAN

trying to see you in therapy
was more puzzling than life
a little broken, a mother not
understood and the child in
me happily wrong. unloading
in the priest's confessional or
in the thunderous silence of the
therapist's office always ended
with damp tissue on the couch
holding discomfort. you my
Jungian guide imagined the
impossible to escort me by
hand to places of basic vision.
you freed forces within me that
begged to matter for all the right
reasons. I once thought nothing is
easier than forgetting then you did
offer me when a young seminarian
a mythical method to uncover the
presence of the Absolute from the
experience of not living blindly in
the world in which a poor mother
abandoned me to the streets. dear
Jungian friend it was worth every
drip of trouble.

THE LIVING ROOM

I saw him drifting into sleep
in the living room, turning in
his chair and occasionally opening
both eyes to peek at the football game
on the TV screen. children played in
the backyard laughing loud enough to
remind people across the street that light
gathered around them. on the coffee table
you could see a vase filled with flowers that
in their quiet way balanced the room and
reminded everyone that in that space no
one would be beaten into a grave, hear
mothers wailing, miss the Cross on the
wall, the elephant in a corner nor the
figure of Buddha on a makeshift table
surrounded by several Catholic Saints
and Our Lady of Guadalupe. except for
the shoes beside the armchair that walked
several countries to get here no one could
say the sleeping man who lived in that chair
was far from God. I watched the game and
smiled at the children playing not far away
and was thankful to have such a close look
at grace incarnate.

FAMILY

a room in the apartment
with a mattress and mirror
on the wall has three kids
in it. a living room with
a new plastic slip covered
sofa welcomes a girl playing
with a brown-skinned Barbie.
a little boy sits at a slightly
open window, he pretends
to cast a line to the sidewalk
to fish dreams. after a long
day of work, a mother returns,
she places the island of Puerto
Rico deposited in a bottle on
a kitchen table. an old record
player spins salsa music. an
abuelita enters the living room
holding a worn rosary in her hand
and mumbling prayers. a candle
is lighted on a bedroom altar by
the mother in this family called
spics by white folks.

LAST DAYS

on the last days of the earth
will you still toss venomous
words at people you thought
not human enough. will you
not bother to find out why our
dreams drink coffee with us,
abuelas gossip at the kitchen
table and children gaze at
the evening stars imagining
the forthcoming of things. we
are nearer to the time when you
will have nothing more to say,
leggy birds will turn away from
you to sing about what happens
and share God's music with the
ones you believed unworthy to
live. on the last days of the earth
a whole new spirit will show up
to help people in shadows find
light, the ground will break up,
crosses will lift from shoulders
and the broken hearted among
my people will at last hear every
stone speak.

DRUMS

congas were struck in
the little park by eight
notable elderly men. we
gathered around them
to sing of the joys and
storms fancy violins on
the white side of town had
not ever imagined. between
each note slapped listeners
stumbled into the places
in them wretchedly silent
while congas made up life
a beat at a time. no one had
a reason to feel incomplete
and everyone noticed a butterfly
land on Tito's shoulder to hear
the drumming lifting the all
darkness.

TOY BOAT

we rode the subway to Manhattan
carrying a toy boat to float with a
lighted candle for the Central Park
Lake like experienced sailors. the
toy drifted for days in a bathtub
and was pushed around by Joey's
calm hand. gently, we launched it
with a string tied to its bow, while
wind pulled it away from the shore
with everything in us then existing.
we sailed the entire morning kissing
the wind, observing the tiny vessel
with eager eyes, pretending the lake
was a bowl of Holy water, laughing
about the toy's navigation on an
imagined rough sea and agreeing
we no longer needed to crave a
blessing or wonder whether or not
heaven could find us.

TIMES SQUARE

I remember discovering this
street five decades ago, the
sight of buildings with bright
lights, pigeons parading on
Broadway, old men holding
brown bags hiding beer cans
whistling at girls and hustlers
in front of a military surplus
store turning tricks. I never
saw a privileged class face
from the Upper East Side on
the pedestrian jammed streets
around Times Square taking
the time to teach kids like me
wisdom lessons. the brick
walls lining the sidewalks are
silent witnesses to the tourists,
drunks, addicts, jons, cops and
escorts. I roamed the Times Square
streets entertained by its pounding
life, dashing billboards, unashamed
lovers and out loud dreamers. Times
Square wisdom crammed into my
soul and it never leaves me, so on
occasion I drop to a knee when in
the area to recall how loneliness was
driven away from throwaway kids
like me.

WINTER

yesterday, snow dusted
children playing on the
street and dogs shook
coats near clean. trees
wore crusted snow like
sweaters and winter strolled
neighborhoods changing
hearts with the grandiose
silence that fell from the
sky. the complicated details
of ordinary life were set aside
and we remembered life is
good and heaven near.

WEEP NOT

I walked into the Mount
Pleasant night passed the
wall with painted words
saying Oscar Romero Ora
Pro Nobis thinking death
which I had seen on streets
and a civil war is part of
God's creation. no need to
weep for the darkness that's
traveling with us.

POLITICS

politics is the ghastly
crime of the rich against
the frail. today, this thing
is the endeavor of perjurers,
hustlers, and moguls with
vile tricks. politics is not
a heap of voting that is
clean, it is more like citizens
asked to live with grief and
oligarchs with bullshit tales
casting the naïve into the dark
like cheap skiffs.

THE TALK

they talked into the morning
about wanting to escape the
screams that slashed deep, the
bruising schools with flattening
words about the Spanish speaking
kids and single-mothers. they
laughed telling stories about
remaking the city, the coughing
little park trees and God who
retired from creation. a whistle
blew in the alley reminding one
boy of the Bronx boarding house
where kids played basketball
until the evening church bells
and winged Angels appeared
on the ledges of the buildings
lining Mapes Avenue.

VOICE

the curtain was thrown back
in a church on the man who
horrified the world with an
upside down Bible in his hand
for a photo that only displayed
wrongdoing. the stop in the
church came for him on the way
to slamming shut the White House
door on the face of decency and
democracy. this malignant idiot
with fleshy cheeks who emptied
jails of thugs sat twisting on a
church pew while a bishop
called him to acts of mercy
for the vulnerable beaten too
long by his hateful tongue
and policies cloaking the rich
getting richer. the world heard
the words of a valiant bishop
who carried the scars of parents,
workers, gay, lesbian, transgender
humanity, strangers, and ethically
innocent kids who need justice,
compassion and love from the
felon sent back to the White House
who appears to prefer to fill the
earth with the dead.

RAIDS

the young women who
crossed
too many mountains
now working
in a zipper factory
are
fearful of la migra.
they
whisper braiding
each other's hair on
break
with the Spanish sentences
learned in small village
churches
God who is
near
will not abandon
people made
more
illegal and criminal
by the felon
head of
State.
they wonder
about thousands of churches
that claim to know
strangers,
tell their stories in
prayer
why

they look away from the
workplace raids
and are deaf to
loud weeping.
these women
who make factory
owners a little more
rich
were pushed
out of no return
countries and
here
they dream
in a country
with blood
dripping
from
its lips.

TYRANT

when he speaks the truth dies
in public. the sentences that
trickle out of his failing brain
conveys gibberish to keep the
world in laughter. with meaty
cheeks the idiot watches those
who observe him while stigmata
appears on his forehead to spell
for all to see the words cruelty
and lunacy burn bright inside of
me.

THE WICKED

the cruel ones have swarmed
government like a locust surge
of biblical scope, their ideas are
being carried out in many cities,
while the cries of victims are for
them a foreign language. the wicked
old man will never have an innocent
night of sleep in the house built by
slave hands, the walls around the
residence are not high, the screams of
the helpless will arrive in time louder
and louder by the thousands and God
will look the other way when those
beneath the wicked man's feet finally
celebrate judgment day delivering to
hell evil men and women of whom
Dante spoke. the wicked old man
will do what pleases his darkness
and his victims will shout shame to
those who stood on the sidelines just
watching.

REPAIR

they try to put truth in
an iron cage never counting
the cost and glad to scatter
considerable bullshit. they
sit in council tilting swollen
heads reviewing the lies they
tell without shame. they never
admit the waste of greed, the
profits from forced calamity,
the wreckage flung into the
world by the favorite words
of treachery. their monstrous
form of government, fractured
wills of citizens, the strangers
struggling to remove the ruling
leeches from them and the death
made young again by them will
perish and with a little help from
protest will keep the country
from drifting down into the
depths of slime. the confederacy
of the unaccomplished led by the
man gratified by flattery may
keep trying to defeat us with
punishing idiocy but light will
be thrown on his abominations
and America will be America
again.

LOVE

the years have run too
quickly and the melodies
of favorite songs are nearer
to us than the highest places
in heaven. we walked among
the shadows, the fierce green
of a Mesoamerican jungle
and the warming sun to find
countless ways to suffocate
sadness for the simple sake of
exquisite love.

LIGHTS

lights in the mountain
village are unlike those
on Manhattan Island that
delight darkness, while
tourists, street performers
and walkers drift along on
chalk marked sidewalks
smiling at each other much
like a flame passed from one
candle to another. lights on
this mountain are like eyes
wide open in the fifteenth
hour of morning watching
for returning exiles, like the
widows who read Bible verses
when others sleep or like
the tin roofed houses under
glittering stars that mothers
with children were forced to
leave. on this mountain light
is dim and enough some say
to guide heaven to earth.

ROAD RUNNER

the little boy speaking Spanish
was on the playground furiously
rushing up a ladder with the rest
of his friends in chase. he never
scrambled to the other side of the
chain link fence separating the
stomping ground from a sidewalk
where three elderly women stood
with two-wheeled grocery carts
beside them, some with washed
clothing and one other with a
grocery bag showing a ten pound
bag of Carolina Rice. broken swings
for these youngsters with bright dark
faces dressed up by the starched shirts
of Catholic School uniforms did not
mean ruin. they circled the playground,
the child chased yelled always steps
ahead of friends calling to him in two
languages.

SUPER BOWL

it is a late afternoon
and on the Superbowl
field a piano man sings
the national anthem. the
coin toss complete the
two teams that prayed
for victory off the field
command the attention
of the devoted who sit
in the stadium and living
rooms reciting words and
performing the rites rolled
out each year to praise
near immortals dressed
for a game. the helmeted
heads with masked faces
in colored uniforms clash
in a spectacle of ritualized
antagonism. the game today
will make us more for a few
hours with colors in play and
unwrapped imaginations.

¡NADA!

there will be no flowers
on the grave of the wicked
man travelling where God
has a way prepared. the price
he thought never due for the
wounds left on vulnerable
human beings already scream
you are no king. humanity on
the earth will not weep for
his death and the world will
dance in spotlights exposing
his masked friends and the
end to the evil deeds of so
many utterly good for nothing
fiends.

TROJAN HORSE

we sit each day astonished
by the latest news to reach
the public square about the
immensely dishonest days
given to us by the darkest
heart in the White House to
play on political weaknesses
and fears. we are waiting for
the fuming tongues in this time
of controlled chaos making
democracy the latest hostage
of the malignant imbecile glad
to burn down the nation for the
sake of Putin plunder. today, the
language of old religion, moral
decency and truth never speaks
from the evil faces amused about
the terror set free that everyday
makes Legion think it is pointless
to multiply. perhaps, light will find
a way to sift beyond the politician
and the spineless party of lies to
build a new nation from ashes
and dust.

GOD

the bells call the faithful
to devotion each week at
the unchanged dishonest
hour. the facts beyond the
church walls and stained
glass windows are oppressed
by Sunday morning preaching
somehow overlooking God's
claim on the world. in Gaza a
child looks for precious things
from her bombed house, a girl
in Texas two years away from
becoming a teen takes her life
fearful of being left alone if the
family is deported, thousands
of federal workers are now out
of work by order of the callous
minds that sumptuously dine and
talk about how to punish people
they despise. on Sunday stories
about the fear of kings are hardly
read and the near naked man that
dangled on a tree is never talked
about in terms of the fact that he
was monstrously lynched. perhaps,
next week the Word will make
its way into the darkness with
spoken prayers and we will see
the truth dripping into the world
from wounds.

BEGINNING

in the barrio, kids play tops,
jump rope, hopscotch and
tag on the sidewalk, winos
drink Midnight Express on
the corner, sitting on stoops
and the little park. when its
hot the apartment windows
are opened wide, the smell
of marinated chicken pours
into the street, and the elderly
gather practicing a partially
learned language to exchange
local gossip. Spanish wears
the face of mothers who walk
home from the subway station
talking about the wind that
rattles tenement windows
and voices calling to each
other in the alley at the oddest
times. on Saturday night a
group of teens gets together
on the stoop cracking jokes,
listening to salsa, forgetting
family grief and streetlights
noisily buzzing to share stories
and dreams.

RESIST

on the fire escape in the
abandoned tenement with
a few friends imagining
a future already denied
by the law of those who
rule marginal places in
the city, it was never more
clear to me that no matter the
beatings, the hateful words
or outlawing magniloquence
of the house in the nation's
capital built by the enslaved
a necessary condition for light
is resistance. we will march in
rage until the malignant imbecile
elevated to high office without
merit experiences the majesty
of those his bootlickers try to
plant in the dark. we the people
with darker skin, the homeless,
the jobless, the undocumented,
the refugees, the exiles, speakers
of other tongues, the detested
and disposable scarred by white
supremacy who carry the weight
of dreams will rise no matter how
many ways the criminals in power
try to slice life up for us.

MORNING

the morning is a gift unfolding
with the gentle songs of birds
perched after flight on the trees
lining the street. these feathered
creatures are messengers come
to us with a unique alphabet
known to them from the heavens,
the mysteries for which swallows
spin in the sky and the reasons
why no one should be worn out
by evil, ever. today, imperfect
humanity will find ways to rejoice
in good news.

THE FIRE

a nation of sheep finding
solace grazing on the grass
is blind to the wall on the
southern border and wolves
leading it to the places where
dreams are slaughtered. the
dull brain of a vulgar idiot
tells us he wishes for peace
with diplomacy of war, he
offers suffering by pitiless
decree, unending bullshit in
every speech and destruction
of government with the backing
of a white South African whose
sadistic control is delivering a
lengthy list of shattered lives
to history. in this nation of sheep
let's make it clear dictators and
their appalling rich friends don't
go to heaven and history will tell
their story beside that of those
who carried out their plans. not
a single truth will be distorted and
readers of it will choke digesting
the accounts concerning a deranged
old man who hung on to his nation
of sheep though never could fool
the world to keep it from thinking
he is utterly full-of-shit.

THE WRECK

I fear the vast darkness away
from Eden promised for those
who will not stay quiet to the
delight of evil men. I fear the
hands that hang paintings on
the crooked walls of a resort
the child from heaven will not
visit to hear thoughts turned to
prayer. I fear the Herodian thugs
who haul the poor into regions
where light is ended, hope held
captive, funeral pyres fueled with
hate and brutes gorging themselves
with food and all the mammon their
bilious hearts crave. I will never
fear the hunger for justice making
rivers rush through cities, oceans
stand still and darkness beg every
victim for aid. I will always dream
of heavenly light leading pulsing
perilous days into wind, storms and
wreck.

STILL VOICE

I was the first to exit the
tenement on Westchester
Avenue, the voices were
still that morning, dancing
on the sidewalk were a few
pigeons showing off their
gray and white plumage
and unable to find a marble
statue in the neighborhood
for rest. the northern winds
never pause in this barrio on
the way downtown where the
Mayor lives and songs of the
poor full of ancient agony are
not ever heard. on my way to
the Simpson Street station, I
could hear Father Rossi say
God is love so there is always
reason to rejoice but the Pepsi
Cola brothers killed Itchy for a
dime bag of dope, Angel was
in jail on Rikers Island after
getting busted shoplifting in
Macy's signature store and
mothers on the block were
busy doing work reserved
for the despised for wages
even that God the church has
made would say secures more
dried up dreams

MERCY

come morning, she will leave
for another world with a kindly
faced autocrat who has the front
door to his nation with a large
prison open for the wretched
innocent, gang members and
the out of luck. she will walk
streets believed too good to be
seen one among the murderous
places by those who denounce
brutality in the name of human
rights. come evening after she
departs, I will lay awake in the
dark, think about the years of
waving goodbye, the village
poor fleeing and the tears that
left puddles on streets. come
evening, I will lose sleep recalling
the silence in a near empty barrio
when fighting came to the city,
tears will pour down my cheeks
as a procession of martyred faces
still ignored in my birth country
marches in my sleep. tonight, I
sigh about the distance and
offer prayers with a language
that simply cannot name the
revulsion that drove her from
a country named in tribute to
a Crucified Savior. tonight, I

may even pray the Rosary that
promises to deliver blessings
to the family members who
were left behind, the frail elder,
and the dutiful daughter who in
exile never stops talking to
God.

SOLDIER

a soldier fell today
in someone's war,
too near the age his
mother kissed him
each night to sleep.
he bled to death for
ignoble greed and his
memory now is not
properly told though
now in earth his soul
walks home. sadly, the
storied website at Arlington
was ordered clean by a
white man with a rap
sheet wearing tanner
paste on a sagging face
and hissing like a snake
dangling in a tree over
fields littered with dry
bones.

AMΣN

the world was intact
when the kids played
jacks in the hallway,
round-up-tag on the
sidewalks, jump rope
in front of the holocaust
survivors' apartment
and when the abuelitas
leaned out of windows
to shout names. the old
men knocked beats out
on milk crates that opened
flowers on fire escapes
and they sang for hours
about the beginning of
time. the world was intact
when Cuca sang holiness
to her boy drinking Colt
.45 on the building stoop
and whenever he put down
the bottle in a brown bag
to hug her. when they ask
will the earth pour wine
and break bread for prayers
it has not yet heard what
will you say?

GAZA

the shelling has not
ended though they
cannot hear it in the
home of the alleged
brave with a felon for
a president. mercy
got lost on the way to
Palestine, the land is
occupied, and Israeli
museums display the
remains of children taken
from the pitiless rubble
in Gaza. those who live
tell their story to colonizers,
occupiers, and American
legislators who never look
heaven in the eye and see to
it that dust in a broken world
never clears. what God do
you talk about to the infant
who only lived a week, the
human beings bleeding on the
run, and death spreading every
day in Gaza and occupied West
Bank?

SANTA

on a cold New York day
after a long subway ride to
34th Street in a city block
department store I met the
real Santa. he filled the old
store with gifts and smiled
at the kids that could see
duty, peace and care on his
fat ruddy face. I wondered
how many apartments had
old Saint Nick visited, how
many cookies had he eaten,
how many notes he left to
little boys no BB guns to
make little sisters fear and
who among the kids in the
Bronx would never see him
and spread their news that
there isn't any Santa Claus
no matter what Mamacita
says. I posed for a picture
with two siblings and it was
hung on Christmas eve on
a kitchen wall and though
we had no stockings to
be filled the photo was
considered by us the best
of gifts. now, when I fancy
the image I swear getting
a glimpse of the real Santa

who drops yearly gifts and
dashes at the oddest hours
with his sleigh across the
Bronx sky.

THE LAND

we should have a land of
kindness near the word of
God, slamming doors on
the syntax of hate, a land
of gentle love for the many
colored hands in which flags
wave. we should have a land
where the sign of the cross is
made wherever people make
it cold saying unlike is wrong
and non-white a crime. on this
land the rich alone should not
wine and sing, poor school kids
should be educated and fed, the
elderly with thinning hair not a
penny cut from their years of
hard work and marriage equality
not a hate crime cause. on this
land flesh, bone and blood ought
to be enough for this earth with
clearer pity to work for justice and
against the tyrants who prefer history
made white.

PRISON

in this nation of many tongues
you lived on the edge of things
condemned to days of misery,
painfully raising your voice in
schools that never got you and
daring in the name of the country
of your birth to protest against the
denial that you are home. I saw
you carried away to reform school
for sneaking into the back of a train
down by the little creek, getting in a
wagon full of toilet paper and tossing
it around like snowballs until the cops
came around. your childhood mischief
interpreted by the white cops started
you on a life of petty crime that led
you into months in detention and to
the sight of your mother's tears left on
a courtroom floor. those who love to
spend their time condemning Black
and Brown kids are the same people
who look the other way when convicted
felons get elected president and rich white
men laugh about the suffering of the poor
while delivering injustice to them.

MADRE

I am writing to you
fifty years later from
a place miles away
from the block said
to have Angels on the
rooftop on sleepless
nights, singing. after,
too many years silent
I am writing recalling
a visit to your new life,
childhood cruelties set
aside and forgiveness
initiated with prayer. I
am writing to you after
celebrating a birthday
with a family you once
met, recalling we sat
looking at pictures I had
not seen for decades and
shared your oldest boy had
died. it is hard to describe
how with a mouth full of
words waiting for amen to
be shouted I finally said to
you dear mother I love you
and want you to be at peace.
you see, whatever happened
we were joined for a few years
until you passed away entirely
forgiven.

AUTHORITARIAN

the truth was laid to rest
some time ago though it
pled to be printed, talked
up in the evening news and
shared on social media of
various kinds. each day is
turned over to the obscenity
of hate, the daily grind of
crushing dreams and brutally
flattened lives. there are yet
a few with space inside of them
for truth, with hearts aching for
those who are made to suffer by
tyrants who delight in the harm
inflicted on others. there are so
many among us who dreamed
of escaping authoritarian rule
only to find ourselves in a world
of hate speech, unjust arrests and
disappearances backed by nothing
more than gibberish. the truth was
laid to rest the very day politicians
invited us to retreat to the hell of
their creation while the president
and his friends use the flag to gag
us.

THE TOLL

my country, sweet country
you cannot give back the
lives of the enslaved, the
first nations cleansed, the
people unmade on the four
corners of this earth. listen,
let light shine again from sea
to sea on people who made
your history, own the slices
of your cherished dream and
invented America with certainty
like the sky over their heads. my
country, sweet country listen to
the grieving silence of citizens
robbed of words and pressed by
the callous rich into the earth in
the name of sin and a future built
on sinking sand.

CROSSING

music poured out of my
trouser pocket like it did
the night your hand was
cut on razor wire placed
in the river you know by
a Spanish name. you cursed
the years of church certainty
guiding you to the border.
with fierce eyes looking
at the distant bank tiki
torches you said would
not ever make you less
human on the northern
side. you know dreams
are not illegal, wicked
people do not make it
into heaven and they will
ask you to speak English
though most of them can
not speak a lick of another
tongue and they parade the
town acting superior. after
crossing you will rejoice in
the good news of making
shadows seek what is right.

SIGNS

a gentle rain started that Easter
night when we shared memories
of childhood good times though
they were few. I never dreamed
you would leave us abruptly on
Walton Avenue, the street that
feared no cops, on the very day
our hearts were occupied by the
story of resurrection. you were
here with your own rather short
story and I have memories and
even a few pictures of you that
whenever they come down from
my bookshelf make me demand
an audience with God. dark as
your premature departure is dear
brother I faithfully crave the future
promised to us by heaven for no
other reason than to sit with you,
again.

THE MARKET

in the market crowded with
people squeezing vegetables
grown from earth's unlimited
gifts, we roam naïve witnesses
to the joys and wounds of frail
life. water drips from freshly
sprayed tables that tell us about
the tolls of peasants in the fields,
their homes, villages and dearest
Saints in the places they visit for
favors. sitting behind a table of
mangos a little girl works with
her mother who is the only one
beneath the Mesoamerican sky
between her and the world that
tries thousands of times over to
close the blinds on the innocent
who work green fields and visit
the aging Cathedrals.

DISQUIET

we have gone for a walk
along the river to take in
the monuments in the city
where the sadistic man who
makes the nation fade before
his blaze lives. what was meant
to be good about government
is perishing in a darkness that
leaves millions of citizens less
confident in the memories they
learned in school and the myths
they are too fearful of repeating
for the ears of the offender who soils
the flag by day and dreams nightly
of improved malevolence. citizens
who have given themselves to this
country are nothing, acts of simple
kindness wasted performances by
the weak and screams from detention
centers and secret prisons at home
and abroad fake. how did we
get to this place where the land is
plotted with suffering and the smell
of death saturates what is good and
leaves people tongue-tied?

SUBWAY RIDE

far beneath the bustling city
streets aged subways clank
and moan rushing into stations
like a great wind to pick up
passengers who board cars
to mingle in many tongues
and colors inspiring hymns
like nearer my God to thee
to fall from the lips of station
performers. riders are going
somewhere in raggedy clothes,
fashionable dress, in their own
heads and past the darkness
and grit of subway stops. when
you come up the steps from the
Canal Street Station you will catch
Mexican women yelling like the
sidewalk was a market place for
wares, you will see a couple of old
Chinese men playing favorite tunes
on an Erhu to gather funds for some
next meal, you will hear church bells
ringing down a street where Little
Italy like Good Friday begins and
you will catch a glimpse of the little
girl exiting with her mother from an
Asian fish market stop brushing
away hair from her eyes to get a
better look at tourists wearing
Qatar tagged gym clothes.

BOMBING

voices have been permanently
silenced with bombs dropped by
the country that killed Malcolm,
Kennedy and King. they were
ordered by the man building
up his bank account with public
funds in the name of freedom
not made for the Middle East
or the Black, Yellow, Brown
and Red humanity that gave
blood, faith and their lives
for it. we are nearer to the
last days with swords sparkling
beneath the sun, churches wordless
with sadness, politicians mostly
applauding acts of unnecessary
violence and looking away from
the fields of the dead and those
weeping by the graves of kids.
the world no longer belongs to
God many say and the bodies of
the dead picked at by vultures are
celebrated by a white Christ's
executioners.

WEEP

I weep for strangers
taken on the sidewalks,
tears water the ground
in an Eden that cannot
find the tree of life. I
weep for the women
and children hiding in
the shadows, afraid of
being in church, parks
and schools, whose very
lives are scarred by White
House greed in this world
that easily looks away from
State backed violence and
a heartbroken God. I weep
for ill children deported to
deathliness and having to
stand in prayer before their
weary graves. I weep for my
country that has lost its way,
for the people who crucify
dreams, and the coffin in
which America is to finally
end.

I CAN'T BREATHE

carry me to the basement
of the church where they
pray in Spanish, where the
candles to Saints burn all
the time, the abuelas visit
to polish altar rails, dust
the gentle face of Our Lady
of Guadalupe and little kids
sit in the last pew laughing
softly. carry me to the ICE
facility downtown, deposit
me on the building steps,
let me anchor my belief in
a Crucified God in front of
masked officials and weep
with me for the troubled in
detention who were dragged,
beaten and unconstitutionally
silenced. carry me to homes
of people not awakened by a
culture of fear with love and
hope running through their
veins.

RUDY

tonight, I will think in the
dim light of my study of
the days we walked to
school in Kingston saying
good-morning to old ladies
with donkeys packed with
sweets for market, making
from banana leaf stems long
leashes to catch lizards paced
like pets and cracking jokes in
the patois picked up playing on
soccer fields with the Rasta kids.
tonight, I will remember Walton
Avenue the newspapers called a
street that feared no cops, the
crack seller that was always in
front of the corner building filled
with the people who were never
detained and Nelly that came to
see you with a kiss. in the dark
silence speaking to me the images
of roaming Orchid beach collecting
deposit bottles tossed, swimming
out to a Buoy pretending to be a
couple of Navy Seals and later
eating shrimp at a City Island
pier will arise one by one like the
pages of an old book. I will spend
time recalling your years of illness,
the Midnight Express that scarred

your liver, the tracks on your thin
arms and the street where addicts
like you give up. I will remember
tonight how inseparable we were
and now the tears I shed for you
keep telling me you do not cry
alone.

THE BEGINNING

I have read the poets who
say do not allow grief a wider
field of sadness in the places
holding sweet memories.
I have read thousands of
times life is too provisional
for the human heart but love
is a thing that conjures mystery,
dances with eternity, and clutches
damaged mourners to rescue
them from darkness. still, your
hour of departure that arrived
without a word is sadder than
others can imagine and closer
now than the unmeasured parts
of the sea. we never heard the
steps made by death without
feet, the knocking at your door
by the collector without hands
and we cannot imagine why death
carried you to a Ball for which you
were badly dressed.

I CRY FOR YOU

death does not discriminate
and it always wants more.
I walked the worst streets in
the country recall the Pepsi
Cola brothers stabbing Itchy
to death, sobbing when I got
the news that Joseph died on
a rooftop with too much dope
in his blood, and with eleven
year old eyes helplessly saw
a man exit a bar chased by two
men swinging baseball bats at
him until the sidewalk was all
bloody stained. I imagined the
ambulance rushing him to the
hospital after he fought like hell
on Southern Boulevard to live
and being wired for monitoring
hoping a last breath was not too
near. I remember my thirteenth
year when a knife thrust in the
direction of my heart was caught
by me in the wrist and I was glad
to have escaped death another day
on the streets that feared no cops
but nothing prepared me for a day
like this one that I suspect makes
even Jesus hesitate with grief. I
wonder when tomorrow starts
without you how I will offer